This Gratitude Journal belongs to:

_____

"Gratitude is not only the greatest of virtues but the parent of all others."

Marcus Tullius Cicero
Ancient Roman statesman, orator and philosopher

The Gratitude Journal

THE
GRATITUDE JOURNAL

Self-Care, Inner Peace & Joy

90-Day Of Guided Questions

---

21 Exercises

Instagram: 21exercises_journals

Dear Reader,

Thanks for purchasing our book.

We feel grateful to serve you with our carefully created:

The Gratitude Journal

& Hope you enjoy, learn and find what you're looking for.

All the best,

21 Exercises

As a little thank you note,
*we've three **FREE** Personal-Growth exercises waiting for you.*

Simply send an email to to exercises21@yahoo.com
Title the email "Gratitude"

And we will send you Three Personal Development Hacks for FREE.

A MESSAGE FROM THE AUTHORS

Journaling helps you to order thoughts, create an exciting future and pay attention to the important things in life. It's a peaceful exercise to help you calm the mind and improve the relationship with yourself. A meeting with a blank page of paper. From which new ideas, new perspectives and new manifestations can be created. It helps you to connect once again with your essence, with the present moment and with life itself. Because your life deserves conscious observation and conscious creation.

INTRODUCTION

GRATITUDE
NOUN / 'gRATiTJU:D/

The quality of being thankful;
readiness to show appreciation for and to return kindness.

There is incredible power in gratitude. It sometimes is being referred to as soft, or being positive all the time. But actually it's a strength, a resilience to pay attention, to be optimistic, and to make the most out of every situation. Even when life gets very tough. Because gratitude is a sure way to influence the release of negative thoughts and emotions in your life. To better deal with worries, stress, and social anxieties. Being grateful gets you right out of your head and into the present moment. It demands that even for a couple of seconds, you return to the *here and now.* Standing still and contemplating life's beauties, your own strengths, other people's kindness' and the gifts you've received in your life. It is fuel for optimism. And it turns setbacks, even the biggest ones, into valuable lessons for life, or at least into a moment of gratitude for the time that has been.

Just like every great skill, being grateful needs practice. Most preferably, everyday practice. This 90-Day *Gratitude Journal* is a remarkable way to practice gratitude on a daily basis for so much as five minutes a day. It may seem short, but over time this could turn into a valuable habit, with extreme benefits. Not in the last place, the benefit of integrating a state of ongoing happiness, resilience, and reflection in your daily life.

HOW TO USE THIS JOURNAL

On every page, you'll find a new day, and a different question. If you bought the print version, there is enough space on each page to answer the question and do some more journaling. There is a specific order in these questions, to give you the best benefit over three months. If you bought the EBook version, you could use your own notebook during these 90 days. We recommend setting a particular time each day for your journaling exercises; for example during your morning routine, or before you go to bed.

DAY 1, DATE:

"Have a heart that never hardens, and a temper that never tires, and a touch that never hurts."

CHARLES DICKENS

Write down three or more experiences that have changed your life for the better. Focus on what it is specifically that makes you feel grateful for these experiences.

DAY 2, DATE:

*"I have always thought the actions of men
the best interpreters of their thoughts."*

JOHN LOCKE

What makes you feel grateful today?
Now, think about yourself 30 days from now.
What would you like to be grateful for 30 days from now?

_____

_____

_____

_____

_____

_____

_____

_____

_____

_____

_____

_____

_____

_____

_____

_____

_____

_____

_____

_____

_____

_____

DAY 3, DATE:

"Do not spoil what you have by desiring what you have not;
remember that what you now have
was once among the things you only hoped for."

EPICURUS

Write down three childhood memories that make you feel wonderful.

DAY 4, DATE:

"Count your age by friends, not years.
Count your life by smiles, not tears."

JOHN LENNON

What area in your life gives you the most joy? For example, family, work or spirituality. And why does it give you the most joy?

DAY 5, DATE:

"All the darkness in the world
cannot extinguish the light of a single candle."

ST. FRANCIS OF ASSISI

Write down three things you like about your money situation right now. And write down three things you would like to have more of when it comes to money.

DAY 6, DATE:

"And suddenly you know:
It's time to start something new and trust the magic of beginnings."

MEISTER ECKHART

What can you do today or this week to give other people a feeling of gratitude? What you give, you shall receive.

DAY 7, DATE:

"There are only two ways to live your life. One is as though nothing is a miracle. The other is as though everything is a miracle."

ALBERT EINSTEIN

Write down a list of three or more negative thoughts you often have. Then rewrite these thoughts in a positive way.

DAY 8, DATE:

"It is never too late to be what you might have been."

GEORGE ELIOT

What courageous choice you made as a teenager or in your twenties is still benefiting you today?

DAY 9, DATE:

"I have not failed.
I've just found 10,000 ways that won't work."

THOMAS A. EDISON

Write down three important goals for you.
Now write down for each goal the feelings that you will have when
that goal is achieved.

DAY 10, DATE:

"Do what you can, with what you have, where you are."

THEODORE ROOSEVELT

What makes it special to be you?

DAY 11, DATE:

"Stop choosing the wrong path, when you know better."

ZEN MIRRORS

What have you learned from your struggles in the past?
And how can these lessons give you more self-confidence?

DAY 12, DATE:

"Every new beginning comes from some other beginning's end."

LUCIUS ANNAEUS SENECA

How have you grown as a person in the last few months?

DAY 13, DATE:

"If you want to be happy, be."

LEO TOLSTOY

Write down a list of all the people in your life you feel grateful for.

DAY 14, DATE:

"We must come to see that the end we seek is a society at peace with itself, a society that can live with its conscience."

MARTIN LUTHER KING JR.

Look at yesterday's list.
Write down for some or each person why you feel grateful for them.

_____

_____

_____

_____

_____

_____

_____

_____

_____

_____

_____

_____

_____

_____

_____

_____

_____

_____

_____

_____

_____

_____

DAY 15, DATE:

"You'll never find a rainbow if you're looking down."

CHARLIE CHAPLIN

What conversations you had this year gave you new insights about life/yourself?

DAY 16, DATE:

"Live in the sunshine, swim the sea, drink the wild air."

RALPH WALDO EMERSON

Write down three things you would like do this week
to give yourself a better feeling, without feeling guilty.

DAY 17, DATE:

"In every moment you can discover all the secrets of life."

ZEN MIRRORS

Write down three character traits that make you an attractive romantic partner.

DAY 18, DATE:

"A great many people think they are thinking
when they are merely rearranging their prejudices."

WILLIAM JAMES

Write down three memories where life/God/a Higher Power
really helped you in a surprising way.

DAY 19, DATE:

"In nature lies the how-to for success."

ZEN MIRRORS

Write down three things you can do
to improve your relationship with yourself.

DAY 20, DATE:

"But the cloud never comes in that quarter of the horizon from which we watch for it."

ELIZABETH GASKELL

Write down one small act of kinds you can do today.
And write three others you can do this week.

DAY 21, DATE:

"The course of true love never did run smooth."

WILLIAM SHAKESPEARE

Write down seven or more reasons why you love yourself.

"It is not death that a man should fear,
but he should fear never beginning to live."

MARCUS AURELIUS

Write down seven reasons why you love humanity.

DAY 23, DATE:

"The power of finding beauty in the humblest things
makes home happy and life lovely."

LOUISA MAY ALCOTT

Which people on the planet inspire you and why?

DAY 24, DATE:

"No act of kindness, no matter how small, is ever wasted."

AESOP

When was the last time you surprised yourself?

DAY 25, DATE:

"Is time really moving on, or are you simply repeating patterns?"

ZEN MIRRORS

Write down a long list of all the things that make you smile.

DAY 26, DATE:

"Not knowing when the dawn will come I open every door."

EMILY DICKINSON

What have others done in your life in recent months
that you feel grateful for?

DAY 27, DATE:

"To live is so startling it leaves little time for anything else."

EMILY DICKINSON

If you could share one message in a Tv-broadcast for one billion people, what would it be and why?

_____

_____

_____

_____

_____

_____

_____

_____

_____

_____

_____

_____

_____

_____

_____

_____

_____

_____

_____

_____

_____

DAY 28, DATE:

"Peace begins with a smile."

MOTHER TERESA

Write down a list of things that make you feel happy
about your home.

DAY 29, DATE:

"Great acts are made up of small deeds."

LAO-TZU

What habits in your life give you a feeling of comfort?
What one other positive habit would you like to adopt?

DAY 30, DATE:

"Hope is a waking dream."

ARISTOTLE

What was one small or big victory you had this week?
How did you accomplish it?

DAY 31, DATE:

*"In silence, I hear my special song,
composed on the wings of this universe."*

ZEN MIRRORS

Write down three or more things that other people
can learn from you.

"Life is one fool thing after another
whereas love is two fool things after each other."

OSCAR WILDE

What characteristics do you admire in a person?
How can you develop a characteristic you admire within yourself?

"A man who views the world the same at 50 as he did at 20 has wasted 30 years of his life."

MUHAMMAD ALI

Write down three empowering things you can do to deal better with worries.

_____

_____

_____

_____

_____

_____

_____

_____

_____

_____

_____

_____

_____

_____

_____

_____

_____

_____

_____

_____

*"And the secret garden bloomed and bloomed
and every morning revealed new miracles."*

Frances Hodgson Burnett

What makes you physically attractive? Write down at least five things.

DAY 35, DATE:

"I had to deny knowledge in order to make room for faith."

IMMANUEL KANT

What things would you like to experience this week? And this month?
And this year?

_____

_____

_____

_____

_____

_____

_____

_____

_____

_____

_____

_____

_____

_____

_____

_____

_____

_____

_____

_____

_____

_____

DAY 36, DATE:

"A rigid man lacks the flexibility of mind to dance."

ZEN MIRRORS

Describe the opposite of gratitude.

_____

_____

_____

_____

_____

_____

_____

_____

_____

_____

_____

_____

_____

_____

_____

_____

_____

_____

_____

_____

_____

_____

DAY 37, DATE:

"I am sure there is Magic in everything, only we have not sense enough to get hold of it and make it do things for us."

FRANCES HODGSON BURNETT

Write down two or more memories where strangers helped you.

*"I am not what happened to me,
I am what I choose to become."*

CARL JUNG

What uncertainties you once had, are now gone?

DAY 39, DATE:

*"If we do not find anything very pleasant,
at least we shall find something new."*

VOLTAIRE

Write down three things you can do to improve
your personal relationships.

_____

_____

_____

_____

_____

_____

_____

_____

_____

_____

_____

_____

_____

_____

_____

_____

_____

_____

_____

_____

_____

_____

"...for love casts out fear, and gratitude can conquer pride."

LOUISA MAY ALCOTT

Write down three things you can do
to improve your money situation.

"As we express our gratitude, we must never forget that the highest appreciation is not to utter words, but to live by them."

JOHN F. KENNEDY

Write down three things you did as a teenager or during your twenties, that make you feel proud.

"There is nothing in the world so irresistibly contagious as laughter and good humor."

CHARLES DICKENS

What do other people need to know about you,
to understand you better?

"Romance is the glamour which turns the dust of everyday life into a golden haze."

ELINOR GLYN

Write down five things that made last week worthwhile.

DAY 44, DATE:

"Failure, like success, is the end and beginning of a pattern."

ZEN MIRRORS

Write down three or more things you can do
to reduce the pressure (and stress) on yourself.

DAY 45, DATE:

"All that we see or seem is but a dream within a dream."

EDGAR ALLAN POE

Write down five things you look forward to in life.

"Never to suffer would never to have been blessed."

EDGAR ALLAN POE

Write down five things you enjoy about Nature.

DAY 47, DATE:

"Without music, life would be a mistake."

FRIEDRICH NIETZSCHE

Why is your life a miracle?

DAY 48, DATE:

"May you live every day of your life."

JONATHAN SWIFT

What do you appreciate about your job / your business?

DAY 49, DATE:

"Don't explain your philosophy.
Embody it."

EPICTETUS

What do you appreciate about your friendships?

DAY 50, DATE:

"Everything's a story -
You are a story - I am a story."

FRANCES HODGSON BURNETT

Write down one or more memories of your love life
that made you feel special.

DAY 51, DATE:

"It is better to fail in originality than to succeed in imitation."

HERMAN MELVILLE

Write down three or more compliments that people
have been given to you.

DAY 52, DATE:

"Relaxation can be the missing link for success."

ZEN MIRRORS

Write down three or more compliments that you have given
to other people.

DAY 53, DATE:

"It may help us, in those times of trouble, to remember that love is not only about relationship, it is also an affair of the soul."

THOMAS MOORE

Write down four or more positive thoughts you often have.

"Earth has no sorrow that heaven cannot heal."

THOMAS MOORE

If you would die right now,
what would you regret not being grateful for?

_____

_____

_____

_____

_____

_____

_____

_____

_____

_____

_____

_____

_____

_____

_____

_____

_____

_____

_____

_____

*"It's the grown-up who disciplines himself,
that can safely see the world as a child."*

ZEN MIRRORS

Write down a list of songs that always makes you feel happy and try to listen to at least three of these songs today.

DAY 56, DATE:

"I am a part of all that I have met."

ALFRED TENNYSON

What experiences have you had in recent months that you would like
to experience on a more regular basis?

DAY 57, DATE:

"Very little is needed to make a happy life; it is all within yourself in your way of thinking."

Marcus Aurelius

Write down a list of five things
that makes you feel grateful for your family.

"Dwell on the beauty of life.
Watch the stars, and see yourself running with them."

MARCUS AURELIUS

What lessons you learned in the past are making your life now more easy and fulfilling?

"Is time moving forward...
Or is it you who runs around in circles."

C.W. V. STRAATEN

Write down a list of movies, YouTube videos, and books that make
you feel happy or inspired.
Or that you very much look forward to seeing.

_____

_____

_____

_____

_____

_____

_____

_____

_____

_____

_____

_____

_____

_____

_____

_____

_____

_____

_____

_____

_____

DAY 60, DATE:

"Busy with needing to speak,
we missed the song."

ZEN MIRRORS

How has your life improved over the last few months?

DAY 61, DATE:

"It is bizarre to treat all differences as oppositions."

KATE CHOPIN

Write down a list of seven activities that always bring you in a better mood.

DAY 62, DATE:

*"Perhaps it is better to wake up after all, even to suffer,
rather than to remain a dupe to illusions all one's life."*

KATE CHOPIN

What activities in your life are bringing you the most unhappiness?
And what activities in your life are bringing you the most happiness?

DAY 63, DATE:

"Who is chasing thoughts, will never rest."

ZEN MIRRORS

Write down seven *small* things you are grateful for in life.

DAY 64, DATE:

"Be clearly aware of the stars and infinity on high.
Then life seems almost enchanted after all."

VINCENT VAN GOGH

How can you take better care of yourself in moments of uncertainty?

DAY 65, DATE:

*"The greatest thing in the world
is to know how to belong to oneself."*

MICHEL DE MONTAIGNE

What about the neighborhood you live in makes you feel grateful?

DAY 66, DATE:

"My expectations were reduced to zero when I was 21.
Everything since then has been a bonus."

STEPHEN W. HAWKING

What do you appreciate about the time you are living in?
Write down at least five things.

DAY 67, DATE:

"Before all masters, necessity is the one most listened to, and who teaches the best."

JULES VERNE

What is your Inner Voice trying to tell you in the last few months?

DAY 68, DATE:

"The more we study, the more we discover our ignorance."

PERCY BYSSHE SHELLEY

Write down three special experiences you had this year.

DAY 69, DATE:

"Worrying can't stop the worrying."

ZEN MIRRORS

What time in your life made you feel the happiest?
Write down three reasons for it.

DAY 70, DATE:

*"Everything that irritates us about others
can lead us to an understanding of ourselves."*

CARL GUSTAV JUNG

What does being happy mean to you?

DAY 71, DATE:

"The best portion of a good man's life:
his little, nameless unremembered acts of kindness and love."

WILLIAM WORDSWORTH

What does being successful mean to you?

"When you are grateful, fear disappears and abundance appears."

ANTHONY ROBBINS

What is the relationship between gratitude and manifestation?

DAY 73, DATE:

"You attract what you need like a lover."

GERTRUDE STEIN

Write down three things you can do to feel more compassion for other people.

DAY 74, DATE:

"Simplicity is the keynote of all true elegance."

COCO CHANEL

Write down seven activities you can do to recharge when you feel overwhelmed.

DAY 75, DATE:

"What is time more than a moment?"

ZEN MIRRORS

Write down a thank you letter to the people who have always been there for you. You don't actually have to send it, but just the act of writing this letter can give you great benefits.

DAY 76, DATE:

"Nature never did betray
The heart that loved her."

WILLIAM WORDSWORTH

What are your most precious possessions?

DAY 77, DATE:

"Happiness is a perfume you cannot pour on others
without getting some on yourself."

RALPH WALDO EMERSON

Write down two or more negative things that happen often in your life. Now write down what you would like to experience instead.

DAY 78, DATE:

"What is reading but silent conversation."

WALTER SAVAGE LANDOR

Write down five or more things
that make you feel grateful for last month.

DAY 79, DATE:

"If you judge people, you have no time to love them."

MOTHER TERESA

Your attention and time are your most valuable possessions.
How can you take better care of these?

DAY 80, DATE:

"It is love alone that gives worth to all things."

ST. TERESA OF AVILA

What are positive, encouraging words you can say to yourself today?
Try to say these words to yourself every day for the rest of the week
and see the results for yourself.

DAY 81, DATE:

"To hold on, you need to let go."

ZEN MIRRORS

Love is the way.
What would you love to do every day?

"Have no fear of perfection - you'll never reach it."
SALVADOR DALI

What act of kindness did you witness this week?

DAY 83, DATE:

"Ideas come from everything."

ALFRED HITCHCOCK

What skills did you use today?

"Love lights more fires than hate extinguishes."

ELLA WHEELER WILCOX

What makes it special to be a human being?

DAY 85, DATE:

"A weed is but an unloved flower."

ELLA WHEELER WILCOX

Again write down your three most important goals. Now write down what you appreciate about achieving that goal.

"*Expectation is the root of all heartache.*"
William Shakespeare

What about your health makes you feel grateful?

DAY 87, DATE:

*"Nothing happens to anybody
which he is not fitted by nature to bear."*

MARCUS AURELIUS

What beauty did you see this year?

DAY 88, DATE:

"Life can only be understood backwards;
but it must be lived forwards."

SØREN KIERKEGAARD

What things you've done in the past, still make you feel guilty?
How can you start to forgive yourself for these things?

DAY 89, DATE:

*"Better by far you should forget and smile
than that you should remember and be sad."*

CHRISTINA ROSSETTI

What have you learned about gratitude in the last three months?

DAY 90, DATE:

*"Choose love not in the shallows
but in the deep."*

CHRISTINA ROSSETTI

Write down a thank you letter to yourself,
for all the beautiful things you have done in your life
and for all the struggles you have dealt with so far.

About The Authors

We are creating awareness journals with guided questions for self-reflection. The powerful writing prompts are designed to challenge & calm the mind and provoke your intuition. We always include questions to help you improve your life with simple & actionable steps.

People have called our journals: *"truly thought-provoking"*, *"original and realistic"*, *"good for finding inner peace"*, and *"therapeutic"*.

Every day we are striving to create the best guided journals in both original content and design, to keep supporting you with your personal growth.

We'd love to hear your ideas, tips, and questions. Let us know at exercises21@yahoo.com

And you can follow us on Instagram *21exercises_journals*

The Gratitude Journal

Follow us on Instagram
For promotions, giveaways and newest arrivals

Instagram: 21exercises_journals

Made in the USA
Middletown, DE
13 November 2022

14771148R00064